THE 90-DAY GAME PLAYBOOK

YOUR PATHWAY TO CREATING WHAT YOU TRULY WANT WHILE ENJOYING THE PROCESS

JOHN FELITTO

PEARL RIVER, NEW YORK

Woodwright | Press
PEARL RIVER, NEW YORK

Copyright © 2015 by John Felitto

All rights reserved. No part of this book may be reproduced or transmitted in any form or by any means without written permission of the author.

ISBN: 978-0-9961649-1-7

Editing and design by Joanne Shwed, Backspace Ink (backspaceink.com).

For information regarding special discounts for bulk purchases, please contact Team@90DayGame.com.

CONTENTS

PART I: INTRODUCTION AND ORIENTATION 1

Week 1: Welcome to the 90-Day Game 3

Day 1—What Do You Want to Create? 3

PART II: GREAT DAY GAME PLAYS 5

Week 2: Setting the Environment to Flourish 7

Day 8 (Game Play 1)—Pick a Card, Any Card: The Top 10 Spiritual Principles
   for Evoking Your Greatness 7

Day 9 (Game Play 2)—Your Lightness and Energy Menu: How to Play and
   Enjoy Life Today 8

Day 10 (Game Play 3)—Your Great Day Game Planner: What Will Make Today
   a Fulfilling and Satisfying Day? 9

Day 11 (Game Play 4)—The Abundant Mind Mind Game: Focus on Your Riches
   and Successes 11

Day 12—Reminders and Tips of the Week 13

PART III: THE POWER OF INTENT 15

Week 3: The Conversation with Your Soul 17

Day 15—Your Meaningful Intention Statement: When You Are Clear, the Path Appears 17

Day 16—Your First Step toward Creating a Meaningful Intention Statement:
   The Five Jumpstart Questions 19

Day 17—Refinement Step 1: State What You Want, Not What You Don't Want 22
Day 18—Refinement Step 1 Exercise: From "Don't Wants" to "Wants".................................... 24
Day 19—Reminders and Tips of the Week 27

Week 4: Further Refining Intent 29

Day 22—Refinement Step 2: Rephrase Your Responses in a Present-Moment Context 29
Day 23—Refinement Step 2 Exercise: From Future to Present 31
Day 24—Refinement Step 3: Complete Your First Draft... 34
Day 25—Choose Success: Your Passions, Talents, and Values 37
Day 26—Reminders and Tips of the Week 41

PART IV: THE POWER OF DIRECTED ATTENTION 43

Week 5: Directing Your Attention on Your Intention 45

Day 29—Captain's Emotions and Self-Talk Logs 46
Day 30—That Single Essential Ingredient and the Blue Chevy Theory 50
Day 31—Directing Attention through Mind Games.. 52
Day 32—Captain's Appreciation Log: Gratitude and Successes 54
Day 33—Reminders and Tips of the Week 57

Week 6: Mind Games and the Power of Metaphor 59

Day 36—Mental Rehearsal: The Been There, Done That Mind Game..................................... 60
Day 37—Envision the Outcome: Freeing Your David 62
Day 38—Images and the Power of Metaphor 64
Day 39—Planting the Seed Mind Game 66
Day 40—Reminders and Tips of the Week 68

PART V: NAVIGATING YOUR GREAT ADVENTURE 71

Week 7: Navigate Your Intention with a Cool Head and a Warm Heart 73

Day 43—Get Your OARs in the Water 73
Day 44—Meet the Crew 75
Day 45—Paddling to Rumi's Guest House.. 77
Day 46—Carl's Rumi-nation 79

Day 47—Reminders and Tips of the Week 81

PART VI: EXPLORING THE OCEANS OF YOUR EMOTIONS 83

Week 8: Rumi-nating and Inviting Insights to Dawn on You 85
Day 50—Your Turn to Rumi-nate 85
Day 51—Refining Intent: Valuable Guidance Information from Rumi-nating 91
Day 52—When in Doubt, Don't Figure It Out 93
Day 53—The BMW Mind Game 95
Day 54—Reminders and Tips of the Week 97

PART VII: NAVIGATING THE WATERS OF SELF-TALK 99

Week 9: Self-Talk—The Self-Fulfilling Prophecy 101
Day 57—Battle or Befriend 102
Day 58—Carl Is Heading to Court 104
Day 59—Carl's Day in Court 106
Day 60—Your Day in Court 108
Day 61—Reminders and Tips of the Week 114

PART VIII: EXPANDING YOUR HORIZONS 117

Week 10: Revisiting the Garden and Advancing Clarity 119
Day 64—The Weed and Feed Mind Game 120
Day 65—The Finite and the Infinite 122
Day 66— Gaining Further Clarity of Intent 124
Day 67—The Reaping the Harvest Mind Game 128
Day 68—Reminders and Tips of the Week 130

Week 11: Understanding Personal Reality and the Bigger Picture 133
Day 71—Your Personal Reality 134
Day 72—From Judgment to Love: The Rewind, Review, Recreate Mind Game 136
Day 73—Intentions in Context: What Really Matters 138
Day 74—The Great Day Debrief 140

Day 75—Reminders and Tips of the Week 143

PART IX: LIVING YOUR FABULOUS WHOLE LIFE 147

Week 12: Interim Play 149
Days 78-82—Interim Play 150

Week 13: Moving Forward in the Present 153
Days 85-88—Interim Play Continued 154
Day 89—The Victory Lap 154
Day 90—Moving Forward in the Precious Present Moment 159

PART I

Introduction and Orientation

WEEK 1

Welcome to the 90-Day Game

Day 1—What Do You Want to Create?

Jumpstart Questions
1. What do I want to create?
2. What is motivating me to create this?

Jumpstart Questions
3. What talents and strengths do I have that align with my intention?   ....
4. Why is creating this valuable to me?   ....
5. How will I and others benefit from my creation?   ....

PART II

Great Day Game Plays

WEEK 2

Setting the Environment to Flourish

Day 8 (Game Play 1)—Pick a Card, Any Card: The Top 10 Spiritual Principles for Evoking Your Greatness

How to Play: Pick a Card, Any Card
• Each morning, shuffle the deck and select one principle card. • Read the principle and relate it to whatever is going on in your life in real time. • Carry this principle in mind as you go about your activities.
Ask yourself the following questions: • *How does this principle apply to what I am experiencing in my life today?* • *How does today's principle relate and support what I truly want to create?* • *How can this principle enhance the enjoyment of my life in the present moment?*

Day 9 (Game Play 2)—Your Lightness and Energy Menu: How to Play and Enjoy Life Today

Today's game plays will include:
• Pick a card, any card • Your lightness and energy menu

Your Lightness and Energy Menu
Write down 10 or more activities that bring you lightness and energy: .... Add to the list as other activities come to mind. Make selections daily from your menu based on how you feel in the moment.
Ask yourself: • *Which of my enjoyable activities will I fuel up on today to bring lightness and energy toward my creation?* • *How are the enjoyable activities I engaged in today enhancing the quality of my day-to-day life experiences?*

Week 2: Setting the Environment to Flourish

Day 10 (Game Play 3)—Your Great Day Game Planner: What Will Make Today a Fulfilling and Satisfying Day?

Today's Great Day Game Planner
It's great to be alive and well! What will make today a fulfilling and satisfying day? Do the "write" thing, and jot down whatever action steps you'd like to take. .... Highlight three priority actions. These priority actions will take precedence over all others. Then, time permitting, select others from the planner.

THE 90-DAY GAME PLAYBOOK

TODAY'S GAME PLAY CHECKLIST

Place a checkmark next to each completed game play:

☐ Today's principle card selected and engaged

☐ Fuel-up activities selected from your lightness and energy menu

☐ Game plan actions entered

Week 2: Setting the Environment to Flourish

Day 11 (Game Play 4)—The Abundant Mind Mind Game: Focus on Your Riches and Successes

Abundant Mind Mind Game—How to Play

Ask yourself:
- *Do I tend to lean toward an abundant or scarce view?*
- *Is my attention on problems or on what I choose to create?*
- *How will the quality of my life be enhanced by further developing:*
  - *An abundant mentality?*
  - *My capacity to direct my attention?*
- Play the Abundant Mind mind game audio.

Today's Great Day Game Planner
It's great to be alive and well! What will make today a fulfilling and satisfying day? Do the "write" thing, and jot down whatever action steps you'd like to take. .... Highlight three priority actions. These priority actions will take precedence over all others. Then, time permitting, select others from the planner.

THE 90-DAY GAME PLAYBOOK

TODAY'S GAME PLAY CHECKLIST

Place a checkmark next to each completed game play:

☐ Today's principle card selected and engaged

☐ Fuel-up activities selected from your lightness and energy menu

☐ Game plan actions entered

☐ Abundant Mind mind game played

Day 12—Reminders and Tips of the Week

Today's Great Day Game Planner
It's great to be alive and well! What will make today a fulfilling and satisfying day? Do the "write" thing, and jot down whatever action steps you'd like to take. .... Highlight three priority actions. These priority actions will take precedence over all others. Then, time permitting, select others from the planner.

THE 90-DAY GAME PLAYBOOK

TODAY'S GAME PLAY CHECKLIST

Place a checkmark next to each completed game play:

☐ Today's principle card selected and engaged

☐ Fuel-up activities selected from your lightness and energy menu

☐ Game plan actions entered

☐ Abundant Mind mind game played

Days 13 and 14—Free Day Reminder

If you have not yet taken a day or two off from the game, you can. You get two free days every week. You need not wait to the end of the week. Use them freely at your convenience. You can take a game break, practice the basic game plays, or review any material covered to date. It's your call.

PART III

The Power of Intent

WEEK 3

The Conversation with Your Soul

Day 15—Your Meaningful Intention Statement: When You Are Clear, the Path Appears

Today's Great Day Game Planner
It's great to be alive and well! What will make today a fulfilling and satisfying day? Do the "write" thing, and jot down whatever action steps you'd like to take. .... Highlight three priority actions. These priority actions will take precedence over all others. Then, time permitting, select others from the planner.

THE 90-DAY GAME PLAYBOOK

TODAY'S GAME PLAY CHECKLIST
Place a checkmark next to each completed game play:

- [ ] Today's principle card selected and engaged
- [ ] Fuel-up activities selected from your lightness and energy menu
- [ ] Game plan actions entered
- [ ] Abundant Mind mind game played

Week 3: The Conversation with Your Soul

Day 16—Your First Step toward Creating a Meaningful Intention Statement: The Five Jumpstart Questions

Jumpstart Questions
1. What do I want to create?
2. What is motivating me to create this?
3. What talents and strengths do I have that align with my intention?
4. Why is creating this valuable to me?

Jumpstart Questions
5. How will I and others benefit from my creation?   ....

Today's Great Day Game Planner
It's great to be alive and well! What will make today a fulfilling and satisfying day? Do the "write" thing, and jot down whatever action steps you'd like to take.   ....   Highlight three priority actions. These priority actions will take precedence over all others. Then, time permitting, select others from the planner.

Week 3: The Conversation with Your Soul

TODAY'S GAME PLAY CHECKLIST

Place a checkmark next to each completed game play:

- ☐ Today's principle card selected and engaged
- ☐ Fuel-up activities selected from your lightness and energy menu
- ☐ Respond to the five jumpstart questions
- ☐ Game plan actions entered
- ☐ Abundant Mind mind game played

Day 17—Refinement Step 1: State What You Want, Not What You Don't Want

Today's Great Day Game Planner
It's great to be alive and well! What will make today a fulfilling and satisfying day? Do the "write" thing, and jot down whatever action steps you'd like to take.   ....   Highlight three priority actions. These priority actions will take precedence over all others. Then, time permitting, select others from the planner.

Week 3: The Conversation with Your Soul

TODAY'S GAME PLAY CHECKLIST
Place a checkmark next to each completed game play:

☐ Today's principle card selected and engaged

☐ Fuel-up activities selected from your lightness and energy menu

☐ Your five jumpstart questions responses reread

☐ Game plan actions entered

☐ Abundant Mind mind game played

Day 18—Refinement Step 1 Exercise: From "Don't Wants" to "Wants"

Refinement Step 1: State What You Want, Not What You Don't Want
Refine your responses to the jumpstart questions, stating what you want, not what you don't want, or wish to rid yourself of. 1. What do I want to create? ....
2. What is motivating me to create this? ....
3. What talents and strengths do I have that align with my intention? ....

Week 3: The Conversation with Your Soul

Refinement Step 1: State What You Want, Not What You Don't Want
4. Why is creating this valuable to me? ....
5. How will I and others benefit from my creation? ....

Today's Great Day Game Planner
It's great to be alive and well! What will make today a fulfilling and satisfying day? Do the "write" thing, and jot down whatever action steps you'd like to take. .... Highlight three priority actions. These priority actions will take precedence over all others. Then, time permitting, select others from the planner.

THE 90-DAY GAME PLAYBOOK

TODAY'S GAME PLAY CHECKLIST

Place a checkmark next to each completed game play:

☐ Today's principle card selected and engaged

☐ Fuel-up activities selected from your lightness and energy menu

☐ Intention statement—Refinement Step 1 completed

☐ Game plan actions entered

☐ Abundant Mind mind game played

Day 19—Reminders and Tips of the Week

Today's Great Day Game Planner
It's great to be alive and well! What will make today a fulfilling and satisfying day? Do the "write" thing, and jot down whatever action steps you'd like to take. .... Highlight three priority actions. These priority actions will take precedence over all others. Then, time permitting, select others from the planner.

THE 90-DAY GAME PLAYBOOK

TODAY'S GAME PLAY CHECKLIST

Place a checkmark next to each completed game play:

☐ Today's principle card selected and engaged

☐ Fuel-up activities selected from your lightness and energy menu

☐ Game plan actions entered

☐ Abundant Mind mind game played

Days 20 and 21—Free Day Reminder

WEEK 4
Further Refining Intent

Day 22—Refinement Step 2: Rephrase Your Responses in a Present-Moment Context

Today's Great Day Game Planner
It's great to be alive and well! What will make today a fulfilling and satisfying day? Do the "write" thing, and jot down whatever action steps you'd like to take.   ....   Highlight three priority actions. These priority actions will take precedence over all others. Then, time permitting, select others from the planner.

THE 90-DAY GAME PLAYBOOK

TODAY'S GAME PLAY CHECKLIST

Place a checkmark next to each completed game play:

☐ Today's principle card selected and engaged

☐ Fuel-up activities selected from your lightness and energy menu

☐ Game plan actions entered

☐ Abundant Mind mind game played

Week 4: Further Refining Intent

Day 23—Refinement Step 2 Exercise: From Future to Present

Refinement Step 2 Exercise: From Future to Present
Refine your responses to the jumpstart questions, changing any "future-oriented" statements into a present moment "process-oriented" context—in the "now" with plenty of "I ams" and "–ings."   1. What do I want to create?
2. What is motivating me to create this?
3. What talents and strengths do I have that align with my intention?

Refinement Step 2 Exercise: From Future to Present

4. Why is creating this valuable to me?

....

....

....

....

5. How will I and others benefit from my creation?

....

....

....

....

Today's Great Day Game Planner

It's great to be alive and well! What will make today a fulfilling and satisfying day? Do the "write" thing, and jot down whatever action steps you'd like to take.

....

....

....

....

....

....

Highlight three priority actions. These priority actions will take precedence over all others. Then, time permitting, select others from the planner.

Week 4: Further Refining Intent

TODAY'S GAME PLAY CHECKLIST

Place a checkmark next to each completed game play:

☐ Today's principle card selected and engaged

☐ Fuel-up activities selected from your lightness and energy menu

☐ Intention statement—Refinement Step 2 completed

☐ Game plan actions entered

☐ Abundant Mind mind game played

Day 24—Refinement Step 3: Complete Your First Draft

Refinement Step 3: Complete Your First Draft
Stream your jumpstart responses together into one flowing statement.

Week 4: Further Refining Intent

Today's Great Day Game Planner

It's great to be alive and well! What will make today a fulfilling and satisfying day? Do the "write" thing, and jot down whatever action steps you'd like to take.

....

....

....

....

....

....

....

Highlight three priority actions. These priority actions will take precedence over all others. Then, time permitting, select others from the planner.

THE 90-DAY GAME PLAYBOOK

TODAY'S GAME PLAY CHECKLIST

Place a checkmark next to each completed game play:

☐ Today's principle card selected and engaged

☐ Fuel-up activities selected from your lightness and energy menu

☐ Intention statement—Refinement Step 3 completed

☐ Game plan actions entered

☐ Abundant Mind mind game played

Day 25—Choose Success: Your Passions, Talents, and Values

List Your Passions
As you do the "write" thing today, don't limit your lists or mind maps to your current intention. Instead, list everything you are passionate about:
Ask yourself: ● *What draws up strong emotion within me?* ● *What am I most enthusiastic about?* ● *What did I naturally gravitate toward as a child, well before some adult told me that I shouldn't or couldn't?* ● *What stimulates me now?* ● *What passion(s) drew me to playing this game?*

Your Passions List
....
....
....
....
....
....
....
Add to the list as other passions come to mind.

List Your Talents, Strengths, and Skills

Bringing conscious awareness to your competencies builds confidence. Like opening up a toolbox, you will select the appropriate tools to advance your intention.

Ask yourself:
- *What natural aptitudes and actions come easily to me?*
- *What qualities do I possess that enable me to accomplish things effectively?*
- *What skills have I developed over the years?*

Your Talents, Strengths, and Skills

....

....

....

....

....

....

....

....

....

Add to the list as others competencies come to mind.

List Your Values

Live by your values, and you will persist in the actions that support your intentions.

Ask yourself:
- *What is most valuable to me?*
- *What are the values I choose to honor?*

Week 4: Further Refining Intent

Your Values List
....
....
....
....
....
....
....
....
Add to the list as other values come to mind.

Today's Great Day Game Planner
It's great to be alive and well! What will make today a fulfilling and satisfying day? Do the "write" thing, and jot down whatever action steps you'd like to take.
....
....
....
....
....
....
....
Highlight three priority actions. These priority actions will take precedence over all others. Then, time permitting, select others from the planner.

THE 90-DAY GAME PLAYBOOK

TODAY'S GAME PLAY CHECKLIST

Place a checkmark next to each completed game play:

- ☐ Today's principle card selected and engaged
- ☐ Fuel-up activities selected from your lightness and energy menu
- ☐ Intention statement—engaged and refined
- ☐ Passions, talents, and values list created
- ☐ Game plan actions entered
- ☐ Abundant Mind mind game played

Day 26—Reminders and Tips of the Week

Today's Great Day Game Planner
It's great to be alive and well! What will make today a fulfilling and satisfying day? Do the "write" thing, and jot down whatever action steps you'd like to take. .... Highlight three priority actions. These priority actions will take precedence over all others. Then, time permitting, select others from the planner.

THE 90-DAY GAME PLAYBOOK

TODAY'S GAME PLAY CHECKLIST

Place a checkmark next to each completed game play:

☐ Today's principle card selected and engaged

☐ Fuel-up activities selected from your lightness and energy menu

☐ Intention statement—engaged and refined

☐ Game plan actions entered

☐ Abundant Mind mind game played

Days 27 and 28—Free Day Reminder

PART IV

The Power of Directed Attention

WEEK 5

Directing Your Attention on Your Intention

Day 29—Captain's Emotions and Self-Talk Logs

Captain's Emotions Log	
Read your intention statement.	
Ask yourself: • *How do I feel about what I am creating?*	
Rather than describing the emotion, label it with one-word adjectives:	
Date	**Light Emotions** (e.g., engaged, enthusiastic, satisfied)
Date	**Deep Emotions** (e.g., anxious, tired, frustrated)
Direct your attention to the entries above and ask yourself: • *What needs are being met, or not being met?* • *What values are being honored, or dishonored?* Make a note of any valuable information:	

Week 5: Directing Your Attention on Your Intention

Captain's Self-Talk Log	
Read your intention statement.	
Ask yourself: • *What am I saying to myself about what I am creating?*	
Write down your self-talk:	
Date	**Self-Talk and Beliefs in Alignment with Intent** (e.g., "I'm making great strides," "I can see that my plans are coming together," "I'm living my dream!")
Date	**Self-Talk and Beliefs Incongruent with Intent** (e.g., "I can't do this," "This will never work out," "Why bother?")
Direct your attention to the entries above and ask yourself: • *What beliefs are being affirmed, strengthened, or fortified?* Make a note of any valuable information:	

Today's Great Day Game Planner

It's great to be alive and well! What will make today a fulfilling and satisfying day? Do the "write" thing, and jot down whatever action steps you'd like to take.

....

....

....

....

....

....

....

Highlight three priority actions. These priority actions will take precedence over all others. Then, time permitting, select others from the planner.

Week 5: Directing Your Attention on Your Intention

TODAY'S GAME PLAY CHECKLIST

Place a checkmark next to each completed game play:

☐ Today's principle card selected and engaged

☐ Fuel-up activities selected from your lightness and energy menu

☐ Intention statement—engaged and refined

☐ Feelings and self-talk entered in captain's logs

☐ Game plan actions entered

☐ Abundant Mind mind game played

Day 30—That Single Essential Ingredient and the Blue Chevy Theory

Today's Great Day Game Planner
It's great to be alive and well! What will make today a fulfilling and satisfying day? Do the "write" thing, and jot down whatever action steps you'd like to take.   ....   Highlight three priority actions. These priority actions will take precedence over all others. Then, time permitting, select others from the planner.

Week 5: Directing Your Attention on Your Intention

TODAY'S GAME PLAY CHECKLIST

Place a checkmark next to each completed game play:

☐ Today's principle card selected and engaged

☐ Fuel-up activities selected from your lightness and energy menu

☐ Intention statement—engaged and refined

☐ Feelings and self-talk entered in captain's logs

☐ Game plan actions entered

☐ Abundant Mind mind game played

Day 31—Directing Attention through Mind Games

Today's Great Day Game Planner
It's great to be alive and well! What will make today a fulfilling and satisfying day? Do the "write" thing, and jot down whatever action steps you'd like to take. .... Highlight three priority actions. These priority actions will take precedence over all others. Then, time permitting, select others from the planner.

Week 5: Directing Your Attention on Your Intention

TODAY'S GAME PLAY CHECKLIST

Place a checkmark next to each completed game play:

☐ Today's principle card selected and engaged

☐ Fuel-up activities selected from your lightness and energy menu

☐ Intention statement—engaged and refined

☐ Feelings and self-talk entered in captain's logs

☐ Game plan actions entered

☐ Abundant Mind mind game played

Day 32—Captain's Appreciation Log: Gratitude and Successes

Captain's Appreciation Log		
Appreciate the riches present within your fabulous life, and acknowledge yourself and your progress.		
Date	**Gratitude** (whatever you are appreciating in the moment)	**Successes** (actions taken that are contributing toward your meaningful intention)

Week 5: Directing Your Attention on Your Intention

Captain's Appreciation Log
Direct your attention to the entries above and ask yourself: - *What needs are being met?* - *What values are being honored?* Make a note of any valuable information:

Today's Great Day Game Planner
It's great to be alive and well! What will make today a fulfilling and satisfying day? Do the "write" thing, and jot down whatever action steps you'd like to take. .... Highlight three priority actions. These priority actions will take precedence over all others. Then, time permitting, select others from the planner.

THE 90-DAY GAME PLAYBOOK

TODAY'S GAME PLAY CHECKLIST

Place a checkmark next to each completed game play:

☐ Today's principle card selected and engaged

☐ Fuel-up activities selected from your lightness and energy menu

☐ Intention statement—engaged and refined

☐ Feelings, self-talk, and appreciation entered in captain's logs

☐ Game plan actions entered

☐ Abundant Mind mind game played

Week 5: Directing Your Attention on Your Intention

Day 33—Reminders and Tips of the Week

Today's Great Day Game Planner
It's great to be alive and well! What will make today a fulfilling and satisfying day? Do the "write" thing, and jot down whatever action steps you'd like to take. .... Highlight three priority actions. These priority actions will take precedence over all others. Then, time permitting, select others from the planner.

THE 90-DAY GAME PLAYBOOK

TODAY'S GAME PLAY CHECKLIST

Place a checkmark next to each completed game play:

☐ Today's principle card selected and engaged

☐ Fuel-up activities selected from your lightness and energy menu

☐ Intention statement—engaged and refined

☐ Feelings, self-talk, and appreciation entered in captain's logs

☐ Game plan actions entered

☐ Abundant Mind mind game played

Days 34 and 35—Free Day Reminder

WEEK 6

Mind Games and the Power of Metaphor

Day 36—Mental Rehearsal: The Been There, Done That Mind Game

Today's Great Day Game Planner
It's great to be alive and well! What will make today a fulfilling and satisfying day? Do the "write" thing, and jot down whatever action steps you'd like to take. ....
Highlight three priority actions. These priority actions will take precedence over all others. Then, time permitting, select others from the planner.

Week 6: Mind Games and the Power of Metaphor

TODAY'S GAME PLAY CHECKLIST

Place a checkmark next to each completed game play:

☐ Today's principle card selected and engaged

☐ Fuel-up activities selected from your lightness and energy menu

☐ Intention statement—engaged and refined

☐ Feelings, self-talk, and appreciation entered in captain's logs

☐ Game plan actions entered

☐ Been There, Done That mind game

Day 37—Envision the Outcome: Freeing Your David

Today's Great Day Game Planner
It's great to be alive and well! What will make today a fulfilling and satisfying day? Do the "write" thing, and jot down whatever action steps you'd like to take. .... Highlight three priority actions. These priority actions will take precedence over all others. Then, time permitting, select others from the planner.

Week 6: Mind Games and the Power of Metaphor

TODAY'S GAME PLAY CHECKLIST
Place a checkmark next to each completed game play:

- ☐ Today's principle card selected and engaged
- ☐ Fuel-up activities selected from your lightness and energy menu
- ☐ Intention statement—engaged and refined
- ☐ Feelings, self-talk, and appreciation entered in captain's logs
- ☐ Game plan actions entered
- ☐ Freeing Your David mind game played

Day 38—Images and the Power of Metaphor

Today's Great Day Game Planner

It's great to be alive and well! What will make today a fulfilling and satisfying day? Do the "write" thing, and jot down whatever action steps you'd like to take.

....

....

....

....

....

....

....

Highlight three priority actions. These priority actions will take precedence over all others. Then, time permitting, select others from the planner.

Week 6: Mind Games and the Power of Metaphor

TODAY'S GAME PLAY CHECKLIST

Place a checkmark next to each completed game play:

- [ ] Today's principle card selected and engaged
- [ ] Fuel-up activities selected from your lightness and energy menu
- [ ] Intention statement—engaged and refined
- [ ] Feelings, self-talk, and appreciation entered in captain's logs
- [ ] Game plan actions entered
- [ ] Select and play a mind game today:
  - ○ Abundant Mind
  - ○ Been There, Done That
  - ○ Freeing Your David

Day 39—Planting the Seed Mind Game

Today's Great Day Game Planner
It's great to be alive and well! What will make today a fulfilling and satisfying day? Do the "write" thing, and jot down whatever action steps you'd like to take. .... Highlight three priority actions. These priority actions will take precedence over all others. Then, time permitting, select others from the planner.

Week 6: Mind Games and the Power of Metaphor

TODAY'S GAME PLAY CHECKLIST

Place a checkmark next to each completed game play:

- ☐ Today's principle card selected and engaged

- ☐ Fuel-up activities selected from your lightness and energy menu

- ☐ Intention statement—engaged and refined

- ☐ Feelings, self-talk, and appreciation entered in captain's logs

- ☐ Game plan actions entered

- ☐ Planting The Seed mind game played

Day 40—Reminders and Tips of the Week

Today's Great Day Game Planner
It's great to be alive and well! What will make today a fulfilling and satisfying day? Do the "write" thing, and jot down whatever action steps you'd like to take. .... Highlight three priority actions. These priority actions will take precedence over all others. Then, time permitting, select others from the planner.

Week 6: Mind Games and the Power of Metaphor

TODAY'S GAME PLAY CHECKLIST

Place a checkmark next to each completed game play:

- ☐ Today's principle card selected and engaged
- ☐ Fuel-up activities selected from your lightness and energy menu
- ☐ Intention statement—engaged and refined
- ☐ Feelings, self-talk, and appreciation entered in captain's logs
- ☐ Game plan actions entered
- ☐ Select and play a mind game today:
  - ○ Abundant Mind
  - ○ Been There, Done That
  - ○ Freeing Your David

Days 41 and 42—Free Day Reminder

PART V

Navigating Your Great Adventure

WEEK 7

Navigate Your Intention with a Cool Head and a Warm Heart

Day 43—Get Your OARs in the Water

Today's Great Day Game Planner
It's great to be alive and well! What will make today a fulfilling and satisfying day? Do the "write" thing, and jot down whatever action steps you'd like to take. .... Highlight three priority actions. These priority actions will take precedence over all others. Then, time permitting, select others from the planner.

THE 90-DAY GAME PLAYBOOK

TODAY'S GAME PLAY CHECKLIST

Place a checkmark next to each completed game play:

☐ Today's principle card selected and engaged

☐ Fuel-up activities selected from your lightness and energy menu

☐ Intention statement—engaged and refined

☐ Feelings, self-talk, and appreciation entered in captain's logs

☐ Game plan actions entered

☐ Select and play a mind game today:

　○ Abundant Mind

　○ Been There, Done That

　○ Freeing Your David

Week 7: Navigate Your Intention with a Cool Head and a Warm Heart

Day 44—Meet the Crew

Today's Great Day Game Planner
It's great to be alive and well! What will make today a fulfilling and satisfying day? Do the "write" thing, and jot down whatever action steps you'd like to take.
....
....
....
....
....
....
....
Highlight three priority actions. These priority actions will take precedence over all others. Then, time permitting, select others from the planner.

Mood Elevators
Draw a line or shade in each of the mood elevators to reflect your state of being in the moment.

Emotion	Self-Talk	Energy
Light	Affirming	High
Deep	Refuting	Low

THE 90-DAY GAME PLAYBOOK

TODAY'S GAME PLAY CHECKLIST

Place a checkmark next to each completed game play:

☐ Today's principle card selected and engaged

☐ Fuel-up activities selected from your lightness and energy menu

☐ Intention statement—engaged and refined

☐ Feelings, self-talk, and appreciation entered in captain's logs

☐ Game plan actions entered

☐ Your state of being on the mood elevators assessed

☐ Select and play a mind game today:

　○ Abundant Mind

　○ Been There, Done That

　○ Freeing Your David

Day 45—Paddling to Rumi's Guest House

Today's Great Day Game Planner
It's great to be alive and well! What will make today a fulfilling and satisfying day? Do the "write" thing, and jot down whatever action steps you'd like to take. .... Highlight three priority actions. These priority actions will take precedence over all others. Then, time permitting, select others from the planner.

Mood Elevators
Draw a line or shade in each of the mood elevators to reflect your state of being in the moment.

	Emotion	Self-Talk	Energy
top	Light	Affirming	High
bottom	Deep	Refuting	Low

THE 90-DAY GAME PLAYBOOK

TODAY'S GAME PLAY CHECKLIST

Place a checkmark next to each completed game play:

☐ Today's principle card selected and engaged

☐ Fuel-up activities selected from your lightness and energy menu

☐ Intention statement—engaged and refined

☐ Feelings, self-talk, and appreciation entered in captain's logs

☐ Game plan actions entered

☐ Your state of being on the mood elevators assessed

☐ Select and play a mind game today:

○ Abundant Mind

○ Been There, Done That

○ Freeing Your David

Week 7: Navigate Your Intention with a Cool Head and a Warm Heart

Day 46—Carl's Rumi-nation

Today's Great Day Game Planner
It's great to be alive and well! What will make today a fulfilling and satisfying day? Do the "write" thing, and jot down whatever action steps you'd like to take.   ....   Highlight three priority actions. These priority actions will take precedence over all others. Then, time permitting, select others from the planner.

THE 90-DAY GAME PLAYBOOK

TODAY'S GAME PLAY CHECKLIST

Place a checkmark next to each completed game play:

☐ Today's principle card selected and engaged

☐ Fuel-up activities selected from your lightness and energy menu

☐ Intention statement—engaged and refined

☐ Feelings, self-talk, and appreciation entered in captain's logs

☐ Game plan actions entered

☐ Your state of being on the mood elevators assessed

☐ Select and play a mind game today:

　○ Abundant Mind

　○ Been There, Done That

　○ Freeing Your David

Week 7: Navigate Your Intention with a Cool Head and a Warm Heart

Day 47—Reminders and Tips of the Week

Today's Great Day Game Planner
It's great to be alive and well! What will make today a fulfilling and satisfying day? Do the "write" thing, and jot down whatever action steps you'd like to take.   ....   Highlight three priority actions. These priority actions will take precedence over all others. Then, time permitting, select others from the planner.

Mood Elevators

Draw a line or shade in each of the mood elevators to reflect your state of being in the moment.
 	
         Emotion   Self-Talk   Energy
 	
         Light   Affirming   High
 	
         Deep   Refuting   Low

THE 90-DAY GAME PLAYBOOK

TODAY'S GAME PLAY CHECKLIST

Place a checkmark next to each completed game play:

- ☐ Today's principle card selected and engaged
- ☐ Fuel-up activities selected from your lightness and energy menu
- ☐ Intention statement—engaged and refined
- ☐ Feelings, self-talk, and appreciation entered in captain's logs
- ☐ Game plan actions entered
- ☐ Your state of being on the mood elevators assessed
- ☐ Select and play a mind game today:
  - ○ Abundant Mind
  - ○ Been There, Done That
  - ○ Freeing Your David

Days 48 and 49—Free Day Reminder

PART VI

Exploring the Oceans of Your Emotions

WEEK 8

Rumi-nating and Inviting Insights to Dawn on You

Day 50—Your Turn to Rumi-nate

Rumi-nating on Deep Moods
What is weighing down Libby's spirits?   ....
Is Amy feeling threatened? If so what is the perceived danger triggering Amy's protectiveness?   ....
What is the feeling (that is, the meaning that the crew is assigning to this emotion)?   ....

Rumi-nating on Deep Moods

What need is not being met and/or what value is being violated?

....
....

What valuable guidance information can the team gather from this emotion?

....
....

How will you make use of this valuable guidance information in a way that meets your needs, honors your values, and serves your meaningful intention?

....
....

How has this emotional reaction become a gift to the team?

....
....

Having Rumi-nated, what emotion is now present, and what is the feeling/meaning you choose to assign to it?

....
....

Jot down a few words of appreciation for this mood's arrival:

....
....

Week 8: Rumi-nating and Inviting Insights to Dawn on You

Rumi-nating on Light Moods
What is lifting Libby's spirits?   ....
What is the feeling (that is, the meaning that the crew is assigning to this emotion)?   ....
What need is being met and/or what value is being honored?   ....
What valuable guidance information can the team gather from this emotion?   ....
How will you make use of this valuable guidance information in a way that meets your needs, honors your values, and serves your meaningful intention?   ....
What is the meaning you choose to assign to this emotion?   ....
How is this emotional response a gift to the team?   ....

Rumi-nating on Light Moods

Having Rumi-nated, what emotion is now present and what is the feeling/meaning you choose to assign to it?

....

....

Jot down a few words of appreciation for this mood's arrival:

....

....

Today's Great Day Game Planner

It's great to be alive and well! What will make today a fulfilling and satisfying day? Do the "write" thing, and jot down whatever action steps you'd like to take.

....

....

....

....

....

....

Highlight three priority actions. These priority actions will take precedence over all others. Then, time permitting, select others from the planner.

Week 8: Rumi-nating and Inviting Insights to Dawn on You

Mood Elevators

Draw a line or shade in each of the mood elevators to reflect your state of being in the moment.

Emotion	Self-Talk	Energy
Light	Affirming	High
Deep	Refuting	Low

THE 90-DAY GAME PLAYBOOK

TODAY'S GAME PLAY CHECKLIST

Place a checkmark next to each completed game play:

- ☐ Today's principle card selected and engaged
- ☐ Fuel-up activities selected from your lightness and energy menu
- ☐ Rumi-nated on a deep or light emotion
- ☐ Intention statement—engaged and refined
- ☐ Game plan actions entered
- ☐ Your state of being on the mood elevators assessed
- ☐ Select and play a mind game today:
  - ○ Abundant Mind
  - ○ Been There, Done That
  - ○ Freeing Your David

Week 8: Rumi-nating and Inviting Insights to Dawn on You

Day 51—Refining Intent: Valuable Guidance Information from Rumi-nating

Today's Great Day Game Planner
It's great to be alive and well! What will make today a fulfilling and satisfying day? Do the "write" thing, and jot down whatever action steps you'd like to take. .... Highlight three priority actions. These priority actions will take precedence over all others. Then, time permitting, select others from the planner.

Mood Elevators
Draw a line or shade in each of the mood elevators to reflect your state of being in the moment.

Emotion	Self-Talk	Energy
Light	Affirming	High
Deep	Refuting	Low

TODAY'S GAME PLAY CHECKLIST

Place a checkmark next to each completed game play:

- [ ] Today's principle card selected and engaged
- [ ] Fuel-up activities selected from your lightness and energy menu
- [ ] Intention refined with fresh rumi-nating insights
- [ ] Game plan actions entered
- [ ] Your state of being on the mood elevators assessed
- [ ] Select and play a mind game today:
    - ○ Abundant Mind
    - ○ Been There, Done That
    - ○ Freeing Your David

Week 8: Rumi-nating and Inviting Insights to Dawn on You

Day 52—When in Doubt, Don't Figure It Out

Today's Great Day Game Planner
It's great to be alive and well! What will make today a fulfilling and satisfying day? Do the "write" thing, and jot down whatever action steps you'd like to take. .... Highlight three priority actions. These priority actions will take precedence over all others. Then, time permitting, select others from the planner.

Mood Elevators
Draw a line or shade in each of the mood elevators to reflect your state of being in the moment.

	Emotion	Self-Talk	Energy
Top	Light	Affirming	High
Bottom	Deep	Refuting	Low

THE 90-DAY GAME PLAYBOOK

TODAY'S GAME PLAY CHECKLIST

Place a checkmark next to each completed game play:

☐ Today's principle card selected and engaged

☐ Fuel-up activities selected from your lightness and energy menu

☐ Intention statement—engaged and refined

☐ Feelings, self-talk, and appreciation entered in captain's logs

☐ Game plan actions entered

☐ Your state of being on the mood elevators assessed

☐ Select and play a mind game today:

○ Abundant Mind

○ Been There, Done That

○ Freeing Your David

Week 8: Rumi-nating and Inviting Insights to Dawn on You

Day 53—The BMW Mind Game

Today's Great Day Game Planner
It's great to be alive and well! What will make today a fulfilling and satisfying day? Do the "write" thing, and jot down whatever action steps you'd like to take.   ....   Highlight three priority actions. These priority actions will take precedence over all others. Then, time permitting, select others from the planner.

Mood Elevators
Draw a line or shade in each of the mood elevators to reflect your state of being in the moment.

	Emotion	Self-Talk	Energy
Top	Light	Affirming	High
Bottom	Deep	Refuting	Low

THE 90-DAY GAME PLAYBOOK

TODAY'S GAME PLAY CHECKLIST

Place a checkmark next to each completed game play:

☐ Today's principle card selected and engaged

☐ Fuel-up activities selected from your lightness and energy menu

☐ Intention statement—engaged and refined

☐ Feelings, self-talk, and appreciation entered in captain's logs

☐ BMW mind game played

☐ Game plan actions entered

☐ Your state of being on the mood elevators assessed

Week 8: Rumi-nating and Inviting Insights to Dawn on You

Day 54—Reminders and Tips of the Week

Today's Great Day Game Planner
It's great to be alive and well! What will make today a fulfilling and satisfying day? Do the "write" thing, and jot down whatever action steps you'd like to take. .... Highlight three priority actions. These priority actions will take precedence over all others. Then, time permitting, select others from the planner.

Mood Elevators
Draw a line or shade in each of the mood elevators to reflect your state of being in the moment.

        Emotion   Self-Talk   Energy

        Light   Affirming   High

        Deep   Refuting   Low

THE 90-DAY GAME PLAYBOOK

TODAY'S GAME PLAY CHECKLIST

Place a checkmark next to each completed game play:

☐ Today's principle card selected and engaged

☐ Fuel-up activities selected from your lightness and energy menu

☐ Intention statement—engaged and refined

☐ Feelings, self-talk, and appreciation entered in captain's logs

☐ Game plan actions entered

☐ Your state of being on the mood elevators assessed

☐ Select and play a mind game today:

○ Abundant Mind ○ Freeing Your David

○ Been There, Done That ○ BMW

Days 55 and 56—Free Day Reminder

PART VII

Navigating the Waters of Self-Talk

WEEK 9

Self-Talk—The Self-Fulfilling Prophecy

Day 57—Battle or Befriend

Today's Great Day Game Planner
It's great to be alive and well! What will make today a fulfilling and satisfying day? Do the "write" thing, and jot down whatever action steps you'd like to take.   ....   Highlight three priority actions. These priority actions will take precedence over all others. Then, time permitting, select others from the planner.

Mood Elevators
Draw a line or shade in each of the mood elevators to reflect your state of being in the moment.

Emotion	Self-Talk	Energy
Light	Affirming	High
Deep	Refuting	Low

Week 9: Self-Talk—The Self-Fulfilling Prophecy

TODAY'S GAME PLAY CHECKLIST

Place a checkmark next to each completed game play:

- ☐ Today's principle card selected and engaged
- ☐ Fuel-up activities selected from your lightness and energy menu
- ☐ Intention statement—engaged and refined
- ☐ Feelings, self-talk, and appreciation entered in captain's logs
- ☐ Game plan actions entered
- ☐ Your state of being on the mood elevators assessed
- ☐ Select and play a mind game today:
    - ○ Abundant Mind
    - ○ Freeing Your David
    - ○ Been There, Done That
    - ○ BMW

Day 58—Carl Is Heading to Court

Today's Great Day Game Planner
It's great to be alive and well! What will make today a fulfilling and satisfying day? Do the "write" thing, and jot down whatever action steps you'd like to take.

....

....

....

....

....

....

....

Highlight three priority actions. These priority actions will take precedence over all others. Then, time permitting, select others from the planner. |

Mood Elevators
Draw a line or shade in each of the mood elevators to reflect your state of being in the moment.

Emotion	Self-Talk	Energy
Light	Affirming	High
Deep	Refuting	Low

Week 9: Self-Talk—The Self-Fulfilling Prophecy

TODAY'S GAME PLAY CHECKLIST

Place a checkmark next to each completed game play:

☐ Today's principle card selected and engaged

☐ Fuel-up activities selected from your lightness and energy menu

☐ Intention statement—engaged and refined

☐ Feelings, self-talk, and appreciation entered in captain's logs

☐ Game plan actions entered

☐ Your state of being on the mood elevators assessed

☐ Select and play a mind game today:

○ Abundant Mind   ○ Freeing Your David

○ Been There, Done That   ○ BMW

Day 59—Carl's Day in Court

Today's Great Day Game Planner
It's great to be alive and well! What will make today a fulfilling and satisfying day? Do the "write" thing, and jot down whatever action steps you'd like to take. .... Highlight three priority actions. These priority actions will take precedence over all others. Then, time permitting, select others from the planner.

Mood Elevators
Draw a line or shade in each of the mood elevators to reflect your state of being in the moment.

Emotion	Self-Talk	Energy
Light	Affirming	High
Deep	Refuting	Low

Week 9: Self-Talk—The Self-Fulfilling Prophecy

TODAY'S GAME PLAY CHECKLIST

Place a checkmark next to each completed game play:

☐ Today's principle card selected and engaged

☐ Fuel-up activities selected from your lightness and energy menu

☐ Intention statement—engaged and refined

☐ Feelings, self-talk, and appreciation entered in captain's logs

☐ Game plan actions entered

☐ Your state of being on the mood elevators assessed

☐ Select and play a mind game today:

　○ Abundant Mind　　　　○ Freeing Your David

　○ Been There, Done That　○ BMW

Day 60—Your Day in Court

The Courtroom Exercise Step 1: Observe
Do the "write" thing and write down your self-talk.
....
....
....
....
....
....
....
....
....
What is the prosecutor's case for why you can't have what you want?
....
....
....
....
....
....

Week 9: Self-Talk—The Self-Fulfilling Prophecy

The Courtroom Exercise Step 1: Observe
What rational evidence has the prosecutor identified from your direct experience?
....
....
....
....
....
....
What is the belief or beliefs your prosecutor is investing in?
....
....
....
....
....
....

The Courtroom Exercise Step 2: Appraise
What is the defense attorney's case for why you can have what you want?
....
....
....
....
....

The Courtroom Exercise Step 2: Appraise

What rational evidence does the defense attorney have from direct experience that refutes the prosecutor's case as well as substantiates the defense's position?

....

....

....

....

....

....

What belief or beliefs need to be invested in and fortified to free you from prison?

....

....

....

....

....

....

The Courtroom Exercise Step 3: Respond

What is/are the beliefs you choose to make firm?

....

....

....

....

....

....

Refine your meaningful intention statement with the empowering and affirmative belief or beliefs that you will make firm.

....

....

....

....

....

....

What action will you take to cause yourself to have a new, successful experience—one that further affirms movement toward the realization of your intentional outcomes?

....

....

....

....

....

....

Today's Great Day Game Planner

It's great to be alive and well! What will make today a fulfilling and satisfying day? Do the "write" thing, and jot down whatever action steps you'd like to take.

....

....

....

....

....

....

....

Highlight three priority actions. These priority actions will take precedence over all others. Then, time permitting, select others from the planner.

Mood Elevators

Draw a line or shade in each of the mood elevators to reflect your state of being in the moment.

Emotion	Self-Talk	Energy
Light	Affirming	High
Deep	Refuting	Low

Week 9: Self-Talk—The Self-Fulfilling Prophecy

TODAY'S GAME PLAY CHECKLIST

Place a checkmark next to each completed game play:

- ☐ Today's principle card selected and engaged
- ☐ Fuel-up activities selected from your lightness and energy menu
- ☐ Intention statement—engaged and refined
- ☐ Had your day in court
- ☐ Game plan actions entered
- ☐ Your state of being on the mood elevators assessed
- ☐ Select and play a mind game today:
  - ○ Abundant Mind
  - ○ Freeing Your David
  - ○ Been There, Done That
  - ○ BMW

Day 61—Reminders and Tips of the Week

Today's Great Day Game Planner

It's great to be alive and well! What will make today a fulfilling and satisfying day? Do the "write" thing, and jot down whatever action steps you'd like to take.

....

....

....

....

....

....

....

Highlight three priority actions. These priority actions will take precedence over all others. Then, time permitting, select others from the planner.

Mood Elevators

Draw a line or shade in each of the mood elevators to reflect your state of being in the moment.

Emotion	Self-Talk	Energy
Light	Affirming	High
Deep	Refuting	Low

Week 9: Self-Talk—The Self-Fulfilling Prophecy

TODAY'S GAME PLAY CHECKLIST

Place a checkmark next to each completed game play:

- ☐ Today's principle card selected and engaged
- ☐ Fuel-up activities selected from your lightness and energy menu
- ☐ Intention statement—engaged and refined
- ☐ Feelings, self-talk, and appreciation entered in captain's logs
- ☐ Game plan actions entered
- ☐ Your state of being on the mood elevators assessed
- ☐ Select and play a mind game today:
  - ○ Abundant Mind
  - ○ Freeing Your David
  - ○ Been There, Done That
  - ○ BMW

Days 62 and 63—Free Day Reminder

PART VIII

Expanding Your Horizons

WEEK 10

Revisiting the Garden and Advancing Clarity

Day 64—The Weed and Feed Mind Game

Today's Great Day Game Planner
It's great to be alive and well! What will make today a fulfilling and satisfying day? Do the "write" thing, and jot down whatever action steps you'd like to take. .... Highlight three priority actions. These priority actions will take precedence over all others. Then, time permitting, select others from the planner.

Mood Elevators
Draw a line or shade in each of the mood elevators to reflect your state of being in the moment.

	Emotion	Self-Talk	Energy
Top	Light	Affirming	High
Bottom	Deep	Refuting	Low

Week 10: Revisiting the Garden and Advancing Clarity

TODAY'S GAME PLAY CHECKLIST

Place a checkmark next to each completed game play:

☐ Today's principle card selected and engaged

☐ Fuel-up activities selected from your lightness and energy menu

☐ Intention statement—engaged and refined

☐ Feelings, self-talk, and appreciation entered in captain's logs

☐ Weed and Feed mind game played

☐ Game plan actions entered

☐ Your state of being on the mood elevators assessed

Day 65—The Finite and the Infinite

Today's Great Day Game Planner

It's great to be alive and well! What will make today a fulfilling and satisfying day? Do the "write" thing, and jot down whatever action steps you'd like to take.

....

....

....

....

....

....

....

Highlight three priority actions. These priority actions will take precedence over all others. Then, time permitting, select others from the planner.

Mood Elevators

Draw a line or shade in each of the mood elevators to reflect your state of being in the moment.

Emotion	Self-Talk	Energy
Light	Affirming	High
Deep	Refuting	Low

Week 10: Revisiting the Garden and Advancing Clarity

TODAY'S GAME PLAY CHECKLIST

Place a checkmark next to each completed game play:

- ☐ Today's principle card selected and engaged
- ☐ Fuel-up activities selected from your lightness and energy menu
- ☐ Intention statement—engaged and refined
- ☐ Feelings, self-talk, and appreciation entered in captain's logs
- ☐ Game plan actions entered
- ☐ Your state of being on the mood elevators assessed
- ☐ Select and play a mind game today:
  - ○ Abundant Mind
  - ○ BMW
  - ○ Been There, Done That
  - ○ Weed and Feed
  - ○ Freeing Your David

Day 66— Gaining Further Clarity of Intent

The Essence Questions
Now that I have fully realized my intention:
What needs does it satisfy?   ....
How does it feel to have my this in my life? Express your feelings spontaneously, using single-word descriptors (e.g., exhilarated, uplifted, joyful, grateful, and appreciative).   ....
How do I feel about myself now that I have created this in my life? Again, express your feelings spontaneously, using single-word descriptors.   ....
What benefits am I enjoying?   ....

Week 10: Revisiting the Garden and Advancing Clarity

The Essence Questions
How are others benefiting from my creation?   ....

Today's Great Day Game Planner
It's great to be alive and well! What will make today a fulfilling and satisfying day? Do the "write" thing, and jot down whatever action steps you'd like to take.   ....   Highlight three priority actions. These priority actions will take precedence over all others. Then, time permitting, select others from the planner.

Mood Elevators

Draw a line or shade in each of the mood elevators to reflect your state of being in the moment.

Emotion	Self-Talk	Energy
Light	Affirming	High
Deep	Refuting	Low

Week 10: Revisiting the Garden and Advancing Clarity

TODAY'S GAME PLAY CHECKLIST

Place a checkmark next to each completed game play:

☐ Today's principle card selected and engaged

☐ Fuel-up activities selected from your lightness and energy menu

☐ Intention statement—engaged and refined

☐ Feelings, self-talk, and appreciation entered in captain's logs

☐ The essence questions exercise

☐ Game plan actions entered

☐ Your state of being on the mood elevators assessed

☐ Select and play a mind game today:

- ○ Abundant Mind
- ○ BMW
- ○ Been There, Done That
- ○ Weed and Feed
- ○ Freeing Your David

Day 67—The Reaping the Harvest Mind Game

Today's Great Day Game Planner

It's great to be alive and well! What will make today a fulfilling and satisfying day? Do the "write" thing, and jot down whatever action steps you'd like to take.

....

....

....

....

....

....

....

Highlight three priority actions. These priority actions will take precedence over all others. Then, time permitting, select others from the planner.

Mood Elevators

Draw a line or shade in each of the mood elevators to reflect your state of being in the moment.

Emotion	Self-Talk	Energy
Light	Affirming	High
Deep	Refuting	Low

Week 10: Revisiting the Garden and Advancing Clarity

TODAY'S GAME PLAY CHECKLIST

Place a checkmark next to each completed game play:

☐ Today's principle card selected and engaged

☐ Fuel-up activities selected from your lightness and energy menu

☐ Intention statement—engaged and refined

☐ Feelings, self-talk, and appreciation entered in captain's logs

☐ Reaping the Harvest mind game played

☐ Game plan actions entered

☐ Your state of being on the mood elevators assessed

THE 90-DAY GAME PLAYBOOK

Day 68—Reminders and Tips of the Week

Today's Great Day Game Planner
It's great to be alive and well! What will make today a fulfilling and satisfying day? Do the "write" thing, and jot down whatever action steps you'd like to take. .... Highlight three priority actions. These priority actions will take precedence over all others. Then, time permitting, select others from the planner.

Mood Elevators
Draw a line or shade in each of the mood elevators to reflect your state of being in the moment.

        Emotion   Self-Talk   Energy

        Light   Affirming   High

        Deep   Refuting   Low

Week 10: Revisiting the Garden and Advancing Clarity

TODAY'S GAME PLAY CHECKLIST

Place a checkmark next to each completed game play:

- ☐ Today's principle card selected and engaged
- ☐ Fuel-up activities selected from your lightness and energy menu
- ☐ Intention statement—engaged and refined
- ☐ Feelings, self-talk, and appreciation entered in captain's logs
- ☐ Game plan actions entered
- ☐ Your state of being on the mood elevators assessed
- ☐ Select and play a mind game today:
  - ○ Abundant Mind
  - ○ BMW
  - ○ Been There, Done That
  - ○ Weed and Feed
  - ○ Freeing Your David
  - ○ Reaping the Harvest

Days 69 and 70—Free Day Reminder

WEEK 11

Understanding Personal Reality and the Bigger Picture

Day 71—Your Personal Reality

Today's Great Day Game Planner

It's great to be alive and well! What will make today a fulfilling and satisfying day? Do the "write" thing, and jot down whatever action steps you'd like to take.

....

....

....

....

....

....

....

....

Highlight three priority actions. These priority actions will take precedence over all others. Then, time permitting, select others from the planner.

Mood Elevators

Draw a line or shade in each of the mood elevators to reflect your state of being in the moment.

Emotion	Self-Talk	Energy
Light	Affirming	High
Deep	Refuting	Low

Week 11: Understanding Personal Reality and the Bigger Picture

TODAY'S GAME PLAY CHECKLIST

Place a checkmark next to each completed game play:

- ☐ Today's principle card selected and engaged
- ☐ Fuel-up activities selected from your lightness and energy menu
- ☐ Intention statement—engaged and refined
- ☐ Feelings, self-talk, and appreciation entered in captain's logs
- ☐ Game plan actions entered
- ☐ Your state of being on the mood elevators assessed
- ☐ Select and play a mind game today:
  - ○ Abundant Mind
  - ○ BMW
  - ○ Been There, Done That
  - ○ Weed and Feed
  - ○ Freeing Your David
  - ○ Reaping the Harvest

Day 72—From Judgment to Love: The Rewind, Review, Recreate Mind Game

Today's Great Day Game Planner

It's great to be alive and well! What will make today a fulfilling and satisfying day? Do the "write" thing, and jot down whatever action steps you'd like to take.

....

....

....

....

....

....

....

Highlight three priority actions. These priority actions will take precedence over all others. Then, time permitting, select others from the planner.

Mood Elevators

Draw a line or shade in each of the mood elevators to reflect your state of being in the moment.

Emotion	Self-Talk	Energy
Light	Affirming	High
Deep	Refuting	Low

Week 11: Understanding Personal Reality and the Bigger Picture

TODAY'S GAME PLAY CHECKLIST

Place a checkmark next to each completed game play:

☐ Today's principle card selected and engaged

☐ Fuel-up activities selected from your lightness and energy menu

☐ Intention statement—engaged and refined

☐ Feelings, self-talk, and appreciation entered in captain's logs

☐ Rewind, Review, Recreate mind game played

☐ Game plan actions entered

☐ Your state of being on the mood elevators assessed

Day 73—Intentions in Context: What Really Matters

Today's Great Day Game Planner
It's great to be alive and well! What will make today a fulfilling and satisfying day? Do the "write" thing, and jot down whatever action steps you'd like to take. .... Highlight three priority actions. These priority actions will take precedence over all others. Then, time permitting, select others from the planner.

Mood Elevators
Draw a line or shade in each of the mood elevators to reflect your state of being in the moment.

Emotion	Self-Talk	Energy
Light	Affirming	High
Deep	Refuting	Low

Week 11: Understanding Personal Reality and the Bigger Picture

TODAY'S GAME PLAY CHECKLIST

Place a checkmark next to each completed game play:

- ☐ Today's principle card selected and engaged
- ☐ Fuel-up activities selected from your lightness and energy menu
- ☐ Intention statement—engaged and refined
- ☐ Feelings, self-talk, and appreciation entered in captain's logs
- ☐ Fabulous Five mind game played
- ☐ Game plan actions entered
- ☐ Your state of being on the mood elevators assessed

Day 74—The Great Day Debrief

Today's Great Day Game Planner
It's great to be alive and well! What will make today a fulfilling and satisfying day? Do the "write" thing, and jot down whatever action steps you'd like to take.
....
....
....
....
....
....
....
Highlight three priority actions. These priority actions will take precedence over all others. Then, time permitting, select others from the planner.

Mood Elevators
Draw a line or shade in each of the mood elevators to reflect your state of being in the moment.

Emotion	Self-Talk	Energy
Light	Affirming	High
Deep	Refuting	Low

Week 11: Understanding Personal Reality and the Bigger Picture

TODAY'S GAME PLAY CHECKLIST

Place a checkmark next to each completed game play:

- ☐ Today's principle card selected and engaged
- ☐ Fuel-up activities selected from your lightness and energy menu
- ☐ Intention statement—engaged and refined
- ☐ Feelings, self-talk, and appreciation entered in captain's logs
- ☐ Game plan actions entered
- ☐ Your state of being on the mood elevators assessed
- ☐ Select and play a mind game today:
  - ○ Abundant Mind
  - ○ Been There, Done That
  - ○ Freeing Your David
  - ○ BMW
  - ○ Weed and Feed
  - ○ Reaping the Harvest
  - ○ Rewind, Review, Recreate
  - ○ Fabulous Five

See next page for Great Day Debrief checklist

GREAT DAY DEBRIEF CHECKLIST

Place a checkmark next to each completed game play:

☐ Today's principle reflected

☐ Intention statement engaged

☐ Actions taken and checked off on great day game planner

☐ Remaining actions transferred to tomorrow's great day game planner

☐ Value from fuel-up activities acknowledged

☐ Great Day Debrief mind game completed

Week 11: Understanding Personal Reality and the Bigger Picture

Day 75—Reminders and Tips of the Week

Today's Great Day Game Planner
It's great to be alive and well! What will make today a fulfilling and satisfying day? Do the "write" thing, and jot down whatever action steps you'd like to take. .... Highlight three priority actions. These priority actions will take precedence over all others. Then, time permitting, select others from the planner.

Mood Elevators
Draw a line or shade in each of the mood elevators to reflect your state of being in the moment.

Emotion	Self-Talk	Energy
Light	Affirming	High
Deep	Refuting	Low

THE 90-DAY GAME PLAYBOOK

TODAY'S GAME PLAY CHECKLIST

Place a checkmark next to each completed game play:

- ☐ Today's principle card selected and engaged
- ☐ Fuel-up activities selected from your lightness and energy menu
- ☐ Intention statement—engaged and refined
- ☐ Feelings, self-talk, and appreciation entered in captain's logs
- ☐ Game plan actions entered
- ☐ Your state of being on the mood elevators assessed
- ☐ Select and play a mind game today:
  - ○ Abundant Mind
  - ○ Been There, Done That
  - ○ Freeing Your David
  - ○ BMW
  - ○ Weed and Feed
  - ○ Reaping the Harvest
  - ○ Rewind, Review, Recreate
  - ○ Fabulous Five

See next page for Great Day Debrief checklist

Days 76 and 77—Free Day Reminder

Week 11: Understanding Personal Reality and the Bigger Picture

GREAT DAY DEBRIEF CHECKLIST

Place a checkmark next to each completed game play:

☐ Today's principle reflected

☐ Intention statement engaged

☐ Actions taken and checked off on great day game planner

☐ Remaining actions transferred to tomorrow's great day game planner

☐ Value from fuel-up activities acknowledged

☐ Great Day Debrief mind game completed

PART IX

Living Your Fabulous Whole Life

WEEK 12
Interim Play

Days 78-82—Interim Play

Today's Great Day Game Planner

It's great to be alive and well! What will make today a fulfilling and satisfying day? Do the "write" thing, and jot down whatever action steps you'd like to take.

....

....

....

....

....

....

....

Highlight three priority actions. These priority actions will take precedence over all others. Then, time permitting, select others from the planner.

Mood Elevators

Draw a line or shade in each of the mood elevators to reflect your state of being in the moment.

Emotion	Self-Talk	Energy
Light	Affirming	High
Deep	Refuting	Low

Week 12: Interim Play

TODAY'S GAME PLAY CHECKLIST

Place a checkmark next to each completed game play:

- [ ] Today's principle engaged

- [ ] Fuel-up activities selected from your lightness and energy menu

- [ ] Intention statement—engaged and refined

- [ ] Feelings, self-talk, and appreciation entered in captain's logs

- [ ] Game plan actions entered

- [ ] Assess your state of being on the mood elevators

- [ ] Select and play a mind game today:
  - ○ Abundant Mind
  - ○ Been There, Done That
  - ○ Freeing Your David
  - ○ BMW
  - ○ Weed and Feed
  - ○ Reaping the Harvest
  - ○ Rewind, Review, Recreate
  - ○ Fabulous Five

See next page for Great Day Debrief checklist

GREAT DAY DEBRIEF CHECKLIST

Place a checkmark next to each completed game play:

☐ Today's principle reflected

☐ Intention statement engaged

☐ Actions taken and checked off on great day game planner

☐ Remaining actions transferred to tomorrow's great day game planner

☐ Value from fuel-up activities acknowledged

☐ Great Day Debrief mind game completed

WEEK 13

Moving Forward in the Present

THE 90-DAY GAME PLAYBOOK

Days 85-88—Interim Play Continued

Day 89—The Victory Lap

Victory Lap Checklist	
I have a greater sense of: ☐ Purpose ☐ Self-acceptance ☐ Worthiness **I have more:** ☐ Clarity ☐ Empowering beliefs ☐ Balance	**I feel more:** ☐ Fulfilled ☐ Content ☐ Enthusiastic ☐ Patient ☐ Present ☐ Connected with others ☐ In command and less controlling ☐ Intuitive ☐ Guided ☐ Faithful ☐ Free to choose what is in my best interest ☐ Comfortable with being uncomfortable ☐ Successful

Victory Lap Checklist

I am more:
- ☐ Appreciative
- ☐ Grateful
- ☐ At ease
- ☐ Joyful
- ☐ Graceful
- ☐ Focused
- ☐ Creative
- ☐ Imaginative
- ☐ Confident
- ☐ Responsive and less reactive
- ☐ Flexible
- ☐ Organized

I am:
- ☐ Lighter
- ☐ Calmer
- ☐ Able to see the perfection within the perceived imperfection
- ☐ Seeing more of what's available rather than what's missing
- ☐ Taking action
- ☐ Less self-conscious more people-centric
- ☐ Less judgmental and more accepting and compassionate
- ☐ Better at prioritizing

I am experiencing more:
- ☐ Possibility thinking
- ☐ Empowering beliefs

I now understand that my:
- ☐ Soul has complete awareness of who I am and my purpose for being here
- ☐ Emotions are how my soul guides me to meet my needs and honor my values
- ☐ Self-talk is how my soul makes me aware of the beliefs I am attending
- ☐ Behavior is how my soul navigates in the physical world

Today's Great Day Game Planner

It's great to be alive and well! What will make today a fulfilling and satisfying day? Do the "write" thing, and jot down whatever action steps you'd like to take.

....

....

....

....

....

....

....

Highlight three priority actions. These priority actions will take precedence over all others. Then, time permitting, select others from the planner.

Mood Elevators

Draw a line or shade in each of the mood elevators to reflect your state of being in the moment.

Emotion	Self-Talk	Energy
Light	Affirming	High
Deep	Refuting	Low

Week 13: Moving Forward in the Present

TODAY'S GAME PLAY CHECKLIST
Place a checkmark next to each completed game play:

- ☐ Today's principle card selected and engaged
- ☐ Fuel-up activities selected from your lightness and energy menu
- ☐ Intention statement—engaged and refined
- ☐ Feelings, self-talk, and appreciation entered in captain's logs
- ☐ Game plan actions entered
- ☐ Your state of being on the mood elevators assessed
- ☐ Select and play a mind game today:
  - ○ Abundant Mind
  - ○ Been There, Done That
  - ○ Freeing Your David
  - ○ BMW
  - ○ Weed and Feed
  - ○ Reaping the Harvest
  - ○ Rewind, Review, Recreate
  - ○ Fabulous Five

See next page for Great Day Debrief checklist

THE 90-DAY GAME PLAYBOOK

GREAT DAY DEBRIEF CHECKLIST

Place a checkmark next to each completed game play:

- ☐ Today's principle reflected
- ☐ Intention statement engaged
- ☐ Actions taken and checked off on great day game planner
- ☐ Remaining actions transferred to tomorrow's great day game planner
- ☐ Value from fuel-up activities acknowledged
- ☐ Great Day Debrief mind game completed

Day 90—Moving Forward in the Precious Present Moment

Congratulations!

PLAYER IN COMMAND CERTIFICATE

THIS AWARD CERTIFIES THAT

_____

HAS SUCCESSFULLY COMPLETED

The 90-Day Game

_____   *John Felitto*   *CFP*
DATE   SIGNATURE   TITLE

---

www.ingramcontent.com/pod-product-compliance
Lightning Source LLC
Chambersburg PA
CBHW080940040426
42444CB00015B/3379